Primary Social Studies for Antigua and Barbuda

WORKBOOK
GRADE 6

T0340551

Anthea S Thomas

William Collins' dream of knowledge for all began with the publication of his first book in 1819.

A self-educated mill worker, he not only enriched millions of lives, but also founded a flourishing publishing house. Today, staying true to this spirit, Collins books are packed with inspiration, innovation and practical expertise. They place you at the centre of a world of possibility and give you exactly what you need to explore it.

Collins. Freedom to teach.

Published by Collins
An imprint of HarperCollins*Publishers*
The News Building
1 London Bridge Street
London
SE1 9GF

HarperCollins Publishers
Macken House, 39/40 Mayor Street Upper,
Dublin 1, D01 C9W8, Ireland

Browse the complete Collins catalogue at
www.collins.co.uk

© HarperCollins*Publishers* Limited 2019
Maps © Collins Bartholomew Limited 2019, unless otherwise stated

10 9 8 7 6

ISBN 978-0-00-832498-8

British Library Cataloguing-in-Publication Data
A catalogue record for this publication is available from the British Library.

Author: Anthea S. Thomas
Commissioning editor: Elaine Higgleton
Development editor: Bruce Nicholson
In-house editors: Caroline Green, Alexandra Wells, Holly Woolnough
Copy editor: Sue Chapple
Proof reader: Jan Schubert
Answer checker: Hugh Hillyard-Parker
Cover designers: Kevin Robbins and Gordon MacGilp
Cover image: Spillikin/Shutterstock
Typesetter: QBS
Illustrators: QBS and Ann Paganuzzi
Production controller: Sarah Burke

Printed and bound in the UK by
Ashford Colour Press Ltd

The publishers gratefully acknowledge the permission granted to reproduce the copyright material in this book. Every effort has been made to trace copyright holders and to obtain their permission for the use of copyright material. The publishers will gladly receive any information enabling them to rectify any error or omission at the first opportunity.

Answers available at www.collins.co.uk/Caribbean

Acknowledgements

The publishers wish to thank the following for permission to reproduce photographs. Every effort has been made to trace copyright holders and to obtain their permission for the use of copyright materials. The publishers will gladly receive any information enabling them to rectify any error or omission at the first opportunity.
(t = top, c = centre, b = bottom, l = left, r = right)

p48 Wavebreakmedia/Shutterstock; p49t Monkey Business Images; p49b Hurst Photo/Shutterstock; p50t Monkey Business Images; p50b Pixelheadphoto digitalskillet/Shutterstock.

Contents

1 Government

Student's Book pages 4–20

1 Read pages 4–10 in the Student's Book. Use words from the box to fill in the blank spaces in the sentences below.

government	Judicial	authority	elected	laws
law and order	Executive	laws	power	
policies	Legislative			

a A _____ is a group of people, usually elected, who have the

_____ and _____ to manage the affairs of a

country.

b In most countries the government is _____.

c _____are sets of rules that can be enforced by authority.

d The government of Antigua and Barbuda consists of three branches – the

_____, _____ and _____ branches.

e The function of the Legislative branch is to make _____.

f The function of the Executive is to carry out the _____ set in

place by the Legislative branch of government.

g The Judiciary maintains _____.

2 Complete the diagram with the missing information to show the branches in the Government of Antigua and Barbuda, with their functions.

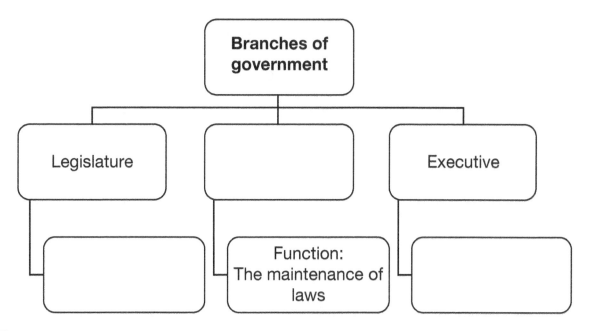

3 Read pages 6–10 in the Student's Book. Then read the statements below and circle either True or False.

a The function of the Legislative branch is to enforce the laws. **True False**

b The members of the Senate are elected. **True False**

c The members of the opposition sit on the left-hand side of the House of Representatives. **True False**

d Ten senators are appointed to the Senate on the advice of the Prime Minister. **True False**

e The members of the opposition are a part of the Cabinet. **True False**

f The Legislative branch is made up of the House of Representatives and the Senate. **True False**

g The High Court is responsible for minor offences. **True False**

h The function of the Executive is to make the laws. **True False**

i The Cabinet meets once a year. **True False**

4 Complete the table below to show which people make up each branch of government.

Branch of government	Composition
Legislative	
Executive	
Judicial	

5 Use the internet to research an example of a service that each of these government ministries provides.

Ministry	Service provided
Ministry of Education, Science and Technology	
Ministry of Finance and Cooperate Governance and Public Private Partnerships	
Ministry of Tourism and Investment	
Ministry of Foreign Affairs, Immigration and Trade	
Ministry of Health, Wellness and The Environment	

6 Read the passage in the box and then answer the questions.

> The government's policy regarding education in Antigua and Barbuda is that all children from age 5 to age 16 should receive an education. However, a number of school-aged children can still be seen roaming the villages and the city streets.

a Describe how the ministries in the table for Question 5 can help the government to carry out the policy. Use the internet to help.

_____

_____

_____

_____

_____

_____

_____

_____

_____

b Write one suggestion you would give to the government to ensure that all school-aged children in Antigua and Barbuda are in school.

_____

_____

_____

_____

7 Write the full name of the following abbreviations.

a DNA _____

b UPP _____

c ABLP _____

d BPM _____

8 You and a group of your classmates are pretending to form a political party. Think of a name for your party. Write the name and then draw the logo in the box below.

9 Describe how the first-past-the-post system of voting works.

_____

_____

_____

_____

_____

_____

_____

_____

10 Read pages 10–15 in the Student's Book. Match each word below with its correct definition, by writing the number of the definition in the space provided.

a voter's ID card _____

b election _____

c dissolved _____

d voter _____

e ballot paper _____

f citizen _____

g Nomination Day _____

h candidate _____

i campaign _____

i   The day when candidates are officially confirmed and their name goes on the ballot paper.

ii   The process by which candidates makes themselves known to the people they hope will vote for them.

iii   The process during which voters choose candidates by voting for them.

iv   A person who seeks election.

v   A person who makes his mark on a ballot paper for their chosen candidate during the election process.

vi   A piece of paper on which a voter records his or her vote.

vii   Shows personal information about a voter.

viii   When Parliament formally ends.

ix   Someone who is a native of a country and has certain rights in that country.

11 Put these sentences in the correct order from 1 to 5 to give the steps taken during an election process.

a   The ballots are counted and the winner is declared. _____

b   On Nomination Day, forms are filed by the candidate

and a deposit is paid. _____

c   Parliament is dissolved and election day is announced. _____

d   Election campaigning is done in the form of rallies, house-to-house

visits and media coverage. _____

e   Polling stations are open and the votes are cast. _____

12 Fill in the diagram to show the steps taken in an election voting process. Use pages 13–15 in the Student's Book to help you.

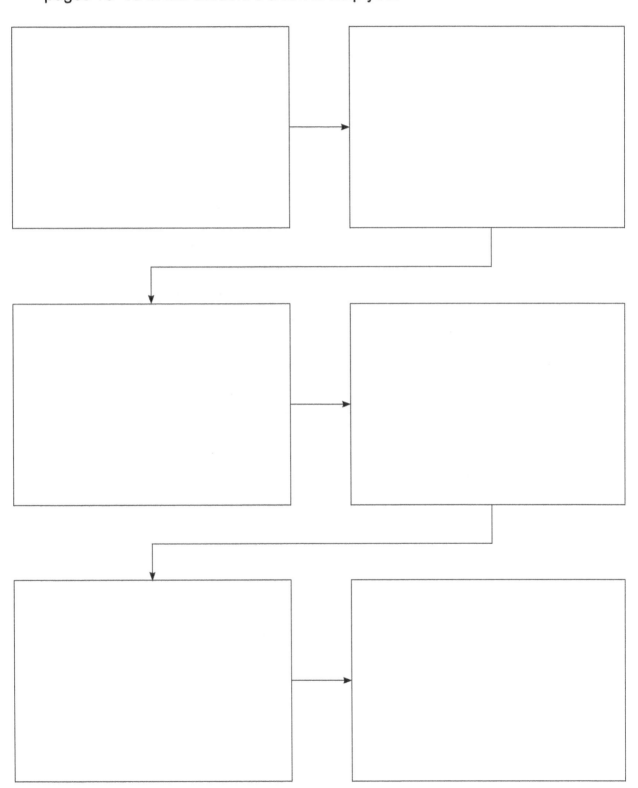

13 Read pages 15–17 in the Student's Book. Draw a line to link each word on the left with its correct definition on the right.

a democracy

b republic

c monarchy

d parliamentary republic

e constitutional monarchy

f presidential republic

g autocracy

i system where the head of state has no power and the Prime Minister is head of government

ii system where a monarch is head of state but he or she has very little real power

iii system of government in which the power and authority lies in the hands of a single individual

iv system where a state can be headed by a monarch or sovereign

v system in which a country's citizens choose their rulers by voting for them

vi system where the head of state is elected and there is no monarch

vii system where the head of state is also head of government

14 Choose any three types of government and give an example of a country with that type of government.

_____

_____

_____

_____

_____

_____

15 In your own words, describe constitutional monarchy.

_____

_____

_____

_____

16 In your own words, describe a republican system of government.

_____

_____

_____

_____

17 Use the internet to help you research three countries which have a constitutional monarchy and three countries which are a republic.

_____

_____

_____

_____

18 In your own words, describe the Westminster system of government and list the important features of the system.

_____

_____

_____

_____

_____

_____

_____

_____

_____

_____

19 Read pages 19–20 in the Student's Book. Complete the diagram to show what the term 'good governance' means to you.

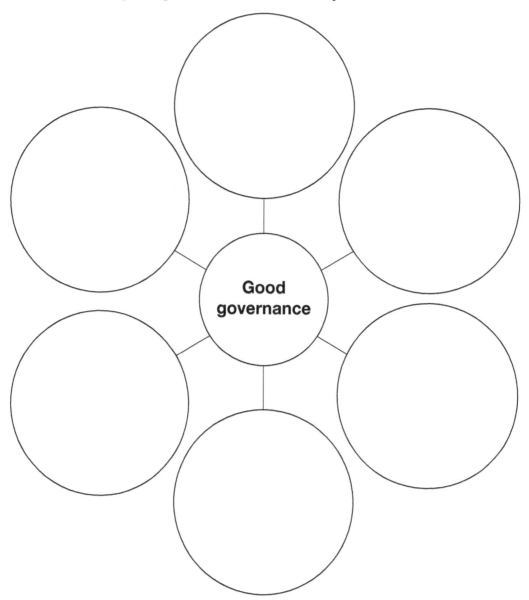

20 Fill in the blank spaces next to each statement with the person it describes from the box.

> civil servant   Governor General   Ombudsman/woman
>
> Director of Public Prosecutions   Attorney General
>
> Auditor General   Leader of the Opposition

a   This person is responsible for reviewing and keeping a close check on the collection and spending of public funds. _____

b   This person is responsible for checking, reviewing and investigating the day-to-day operations of ministries, tax offices, and all other offices concerned with government business, to see if there is corruption and inefficiency. This is done whenever there is a complaint from a citizen.

_____

c   This person is the principal legal advisor to the government, appointed by the Governor General on the advice of the Prime Minister. This person is a member of the Cabinet. _____

d   This person has the right to start, carry out or stop all criminal proceedings.

_____

e   This person is named by the Governor General and is usually the leader of the members of the minority party in the House of Representatives.

_____

f   This person represents the sovereign of Great Britain and is appointed on the advice of the Prime Minister. _____

g   This person is a full-time employee whose duty is to serve the government of the day. _____

21 Put a tick by the correct choice to complete each of these sentences.

a In democratic Caribbean countries like Antigua and Barbuda, general elections are usually held every:

i two years

ii four years

iii five years

iv seven years

b The leader of Cabinet is the:

i Prime Minister

ii President

iii Governor General

iv Leader of the Opposition

c There are ...... constituencies in Antigua and Barbuda.

i 16

ii 17

iii 18

iv 20

d To vote in an election in Antigua and Barbuda you should be:

i 20 years and over and have a job

ii 18 years and over, be a legal citizen and have a voter's ID card

iii a citizen of Antigua and Barbuda and have voted already

iv a member of ALP or UPP and a holder of an Antigua and Barbuda licence

22 Find the words related to Unit I below in the wordsearch.

A	Z	L	A	T	V	B	S	J	G	J	C	K	F	L	F	C	Z	L	E	H	B	Q	R	X
G	D	O	A	O	L	P	N	E	U	C	G	V	A	G	A	O	M	F	B	G	D	W	I	E
L	K	W	Y	Q	A	W	O	D	I	Z	O	R	C	G	E	N	D	I	S	E	N	A	T	E
L	L	E	A	X	K	T	I	U	K	C	E	M	Z	Y	T	S	J	U	N	Q	P	F	I	Y
I	E	R	J	L	V	C	T	T	D	N	I	F	V	F	P	T	T	M	C	I	T	O	N	O
B	V	G	Z	W	I	F	C	P	E	Q	Y	L	A	C	S	I	E	L	O	Q	S	W	S	V
B	K	F	J	A	J	P	E	G	G	O	M	T	O	Q	H	T	N	L	I	N	P	T	B	M
O	L	A	L	G	Q	L	L	V	J	R	E	P	P	U	U	I	Y	D	O	F	Q	E	S
Z	V	M	H	G	X	O	E	G	B	W	R	G	A	K	C	E	B	S	U	S	L	T	H	R
U	G	R	C	S	K	K	D	A	Y	U	Y	X	A	A	Z	N	A	Z	W	E	J	A	B	R
R	E	P	R	E	S	E	N	T	A	T	I	V	E	N	N	C	C	G	A	O	E	G	P
T	N	E	M	N	R	E	V	O	G	I	I	O	N	Q	I	Y	D	I	V	Z	L	H	V	R
B	N	W	O	K	S	W	D	C	J	W	Q	R	S	R	U	S	S	I	G	H	G	J	Q	R
S	E	H	C	N	A	R	B	I	T	D	G	P	O	B	Z	L	A	P	F	P	O	O	P	G
Q	J	V	W	I	E	B	K	Z	J	E	E	M	Q	H	A	F	E	T	Y	A	V	V	O	D
X	E	V	Y	Z	N	I	B	Y	C	M	F	B	K	T	T	V	W	H	I	D	E	H	A	R
T	J	C	P	R	S	B	H	B	O	Q	Y	S	I	W	I	U	X	M	G	O	R	G	E	V
V	S	N	W	W	O	O	K	G	B	G	T	V	E	T	R	P	A	L	D	Z	N	G	V	A
D	J	U	M	D	U	P	R	J	B	H	E	V	U	U	O	V	E	Y	T	O	O	E	P	E
O	W	Q	X	S	Y	I	X	I	D	H	R	C	F	T	X	C	U	L	A	S	R	S	W	M
E	V	H	E	F	H	V	L	M	M	O	E	U	Q	A	W	P	Y	D	V	C	S	G	J	V
S	E	N	A	T	O	R	S	K	O	X	I	O	L	Q	Y	H	P	G	H	O	B	T	D	R

> authority   bill   branches   cabinet   constituency
> elections   general   government   judicial   governor
> laws   legislative   house   lower   minister
> organisation   policies   representative   senate
> senators   upper

2 Citizenship

Student's Book pages 21–31

1 Read pages 21–22 in the Student's Book, then answer the following questions.

a In your own words, define the term 'citizen'.

_____

_____

b In your own words, define the term 'citizenship'.

_____

_____

c List and explain four ways a person can become a citizen of Antigua and Barbuda.

_____

_____

_____

_____

_____

_____

_____

2 Read pages 21–26 in the Student's Book. Draw a line to link each of the words on the left with its correct definition on the right.

a national identity

b citizen

c right

d personal identity

e responsibility

f citizenship

i a freedom that is protected by a country's constitution and is enforceable in a court of law

ii the sense of belonging to your country

iii the concept you develop about yourself that changes over the course of your life

iv someone who is a member of a country and who has certain rights in that country

v the condition of being a citizen of a particular country, with the rights and responsibilities being a citizen brings

vi a moral obligation

3 Jane has been living in Antigua for the last 10 years. She applied to become a citizen and has had her application approved. Now that she is a citizen of Antigua and Barbuda, explain what are her fundamental rights and freedoms guaranteed to her by new citizenship status.

_____

_____

_____

_____

_____

_____

_____

4 Put these rights and responsibilities of citizens under the correct heading in the table.

To obey the laws.

To be treated equally under the law.

To accept that the government has the right to rule.

To vote in free elections.

To be given a fair trial if accused of a crime.

To pay taxes.

To be a resident in the country.

To stand for public office.

To enjoy the modern ideas of civil liberty, such as freedom of expression, association, movement, religion and thought.

Rights	Responsibilities

5 Circle the bubbles which show the qualities of a good citizen.

Staying informed on issues in the country

Taking things that don't belong to you

Refusing to vote

Attending town hall meetings

Believing in equality for all

Disobeying laws of the country

Being loyal to the nation

Showing tolerance of the differences in others

Wasting water

6 What can **you** do to show good citizenship?

a At home

_____

_____

b At school

_____

_____

c In your community

_____

_____

d In your country

_____

_____

7 Isabella is a new child in your class. She is Spanish and does not speak English fluently. Every time Isabella tries to speak in the class, John and Jason laugh at her. What advice would you give the boys about this?

_____

_____

_____

_____

8 Explain two things we can do to show tolerance to others.

_____

_____

_____

_____

9 What are some ways that a citizen of Antigua and Barbuda may protest if they fear their rights are being taken away from them?

_____

_____

_____

_____

10 Select an outstanding citizen from your community and write a summary of the good things that this citizen has done in the box below. Add a picture of the person. If you need more space, use a separate sheet of paper.

11 Select a national hero from around the Caribbean and, using the internet to help, research why the person became a hero. Write your findings below or on a separate sheet of paper if you need more space.

_____

_____

_____

_____

_____

_____

_____

12 Find the words related to Unit 2 below in the wordsearch.

V	N	I	C	G	P	H	G	P	R	S	G	C	N	Y
Y	Y	P	D	M	V	S	A	H	T	F	N	O	O	R
C	T	J	D	O	O	S	Y	H	R	O	B	M	I	T
X	K	I	Y	I	S	D	G	F	I	X	I	M	T	N
X	I	P	L	P	M	I	E	T	H	F	R	U	A	U
F	W	D	O	I	R	M	U	E	A	Z	T	N	Z	O
B	I	R	K	C	B	T	I	D	R	B	H	I	I	C
T	T	Z	D	F	I	I	Z	G	H	F	O	T	L	K
G	E	Z	X	T	N	G	S	B	R	Z	T	Y	A	K
L	P	Z	S	Z	J	B	S	N	X	A	H	H	R	G
V	G	N	D	E	C	E	N	T	O	P	N	X	U	I
L	O	Y	E	W	G	O	K	B	A	P	H	T	T	X
C	N	E	Z	I	T	I	C	I	P	T	S	C	A	O
C	I	T	I	Z	E	N	S	H	I	P	U	E	N	I
C	F	H	Z	Q	H	P	A	Y	K	G	F	S	R	K

birth   citizen   citizenship   community   constitution

country   decent   freedom   immigrant   naturalisation

passport   responsibility   rights   status

3 Agriculture

Student's Book pages 32–46

1 Read pages 32–33 in the Student's Book, then answer the following questions.

a In your own words, define the term 'agriculture'.

_____

_____

b Name the four main types of industries.

_____

_____

c List the different categories of industry found in Antigua and Barbuda.

_____

_____

_____

_____

_____

_____

_____

_____

_____

_____

_____

_____

_____

_____

_____

_____

_____

_____

_____

2 Explain the role of agriculture in the economy of Antigua and Barbuda.

_____

_____

_____

_____

_____

_____

_____

_____

_____

3 The table below will compare features of commercial arable farming and small farming systems. Put features from the box in the correct column.

> Small area for farming
>
> Harvesting done by hand
>
> Monoculture
>
> Crops sold to supermarkets
>
> Many types of crops produced
>
> Machinery used for harvesting
>
> Crops sold at the market

Commercial arable farming	Small farming systems

4 Choose four features for each of 'kitchen gardens' and 'food forests'. Add the features to the ideas maps below.

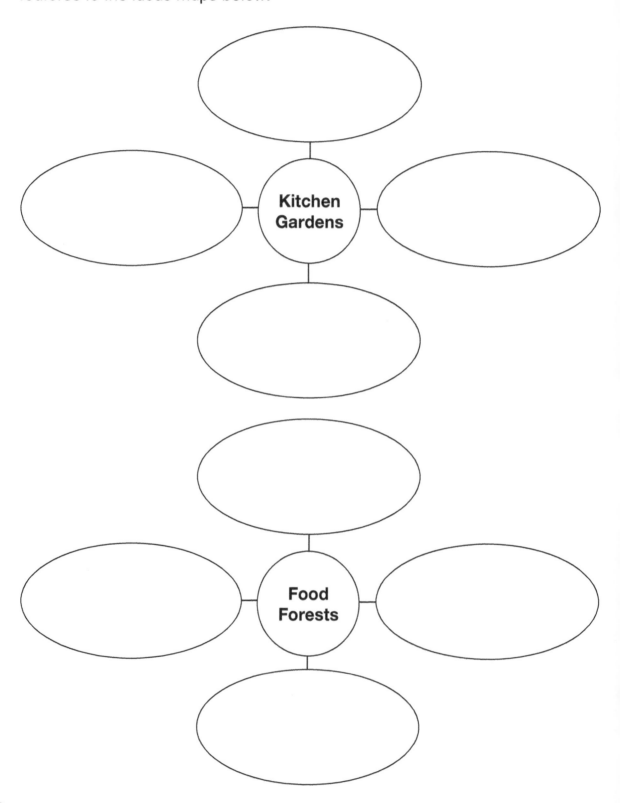

5 What are some of the reasons why you think a person may decide to become a farmer?

_____

_____

_____

_____

_____

_____

_____

_____

6 List the benefits of agriculture on Antigua and Barbuda.

_____

_____

_____

_____

_____

_____

_____

_____

_____

_____

7 List the risks to agriculture on Antigua and Barbuda.

_____

_____

_____

_____

_____

_____

_____

8 Write a list of the main crops that are exported from Antigua and Barbuda.

_____

_____

_____

_____

_____

_____

9 Read pages 43–44 in the Student's Book, about careers and employment opportunities in agriculture. Choose two of the jobs listed and, using the internet, research what the roles involve, what qualifications you might need and where you can do the job. Write notes below and add photographs showing the job.

10 Some people think that agriculture is just for older people and not for younger people. Do you agree with that idea? Give reasons to explain your answer.

_____

_____

_____

_____

11 In your own words, explain what impact globalisation is having on agriculture in Antigua and Barbuda.

_____

_____

_____

_____

_____

_____

_____

_____

_____

12 In your own words, explain how technology is changing agriculture.

_____

_____

_____

_____

13 Read the paragraph carefully then say whether each statement below refers to primary, secondary or tertiary industry.

> Mabel's grandparents have a farm. They grow a lot of corn. They sell roast corn at the side of the road in the afternoon. When they harvest too much, they sell some to Mrs Cornwall who makes 'ash um' (ground roasted corn with sugar) with it. The children at my school like it. Do you know why it's called 'ash um'? It's because if you speak with it in your mouth, you can easily choke.

a Mrs Cornwall makes 'ash um' with the roast corn. _____

b Mabel's grandparents sell roast corn at the side of the road.

_____

c Mabel's grandparents grow a lot of corn. _____

d Mrs Cornwall sells 'ash um'. _____

14 Choose a suitable word from the box to complete each statement.

agriculture   crab catching   fishing   cottage

a Barbuda's main industry is _____.

b One primary industry that is found in Antigua is _____.

c An industry that is done from someone's residence is called a

_____ industry.

15 Find the words related to Unit 3 below in the wordsearch.

G	X	L	T	H	G	C	N	Y	D	T	K	S	G	G
N	T	K	K	E	R	N	M	E	N	T	E	Y	R	E
I	S	T	N	O	C	O	I	E	D	C	A	O	L	N
M	E	C	P	O	N	H	M	T	U	R	W	K	A	G
R	R	S	I	O	I	Y	N	R	N	I	A	H	I	I
A	O	D	C	E	O	T	I	O	N	A	W	G	C	N
F	F	E	O	L	N	T	A	G	L	K	L	O	R	D
T	F	D	P	O	Y	C	F	V	J	O	B	P	E	U
R	E	M	R	A	F	Y	E	Y	I	C	G	H	M	S
B	E	G	N	I	T	F	I	H	S	T	L	Y	M	T
E	R	U	T	L	U	C	I	R	G	A	L	F	O	R
J	V	I	D	H	E	A	L	T	H	B	W	U	C	Y
H	A	R	V	E	S	T	I	N	G	K	X	D	C	O
A	N	I	M	A	L	S	Y	E	N	O	M	X	Z	N
X	L	V	R	M	V	J	T	J	E	X	M	C	E	Q

agriculture   animals   commercial   cultivation

economy   employment   farmer   farming

food   forest   garden   growing   harvesting

health   industry   money   planting   science

security   shifting   technology

4 Map reading and field study

Student's Book pages 47–52

1 Label the name of each group of countries shown.

a _____

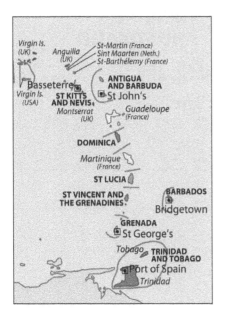

b _____

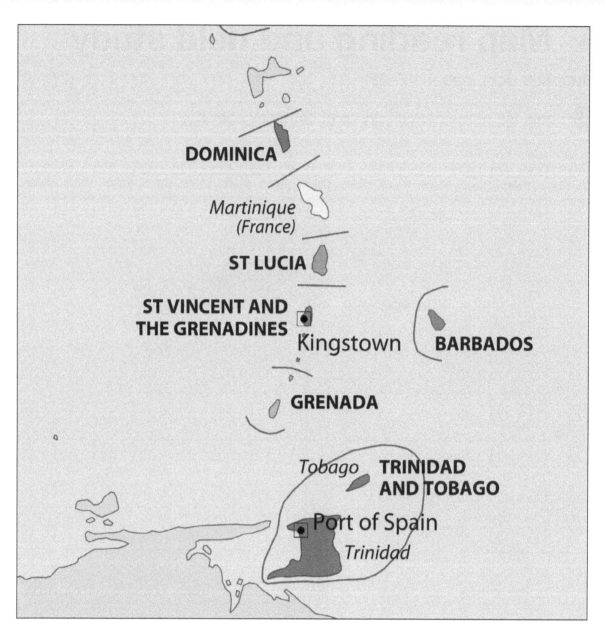

DOMINICA

Martinique
(France)

ST LUCIA

ST VINCENT AND
THE GRENADINES

Kingstown

BARBADOS

GRENADA

Tobago   TRINIDAD
AND TOBAGO

Port of Spain
Trinidad

c _____

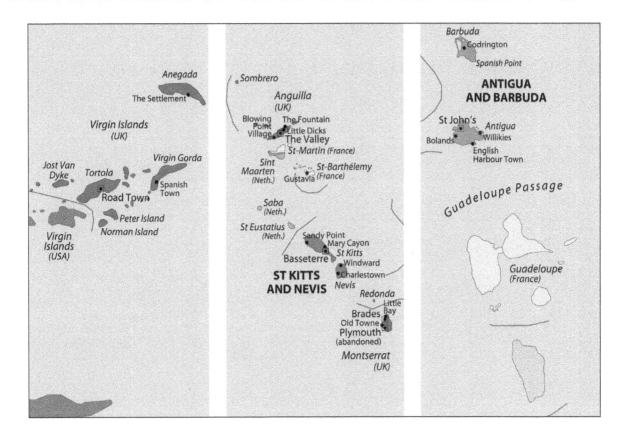

Anegada
The Settlement

Virgin Islands
(UK)

Sombrero

Anguilla
(UK)

Virgin Gorda

Blowing
Point
Village

The Fountain
Little Dicks
The Valley
St-Martin (France)

Jost Van
Dyke

Tortola

Spanish
Town

Road Town

Sint
Maarten
(Neth.)

St-Barthélemy
(France)
Gustavia

Barbuda
Codrington
Spanish Point

ANTIGUA
AND BARBUDA

St John's
Bolands

Antigua
Willikies

English
Harbour Town

Peter Island

Saba
(Neth.)

Norman Island

Virgin
Islands
(USA)

St Eustatius
(Neth.)

Sandy Point
Mary Cayon
St Kitts
Windward

Guadeloupe Passage

Basseterre

ST KITTS
AND NEVIS

Charlestown
Nevis

Redonda
Little
Bay

Guadeloupe
(France)

Brades
Old Towne
Plymouth
(abandoned)

Montserrat
(UK)

d _____

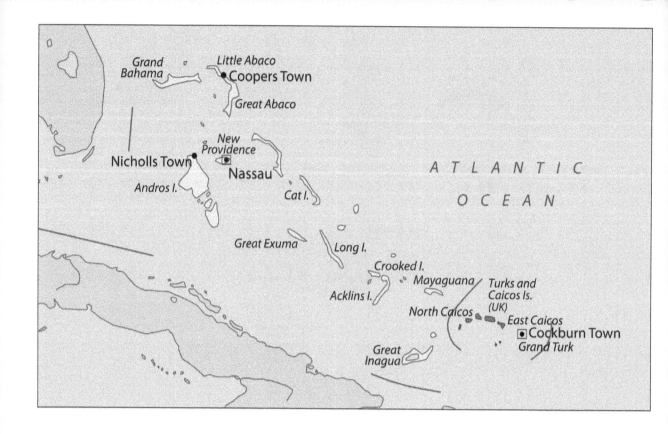

e _____

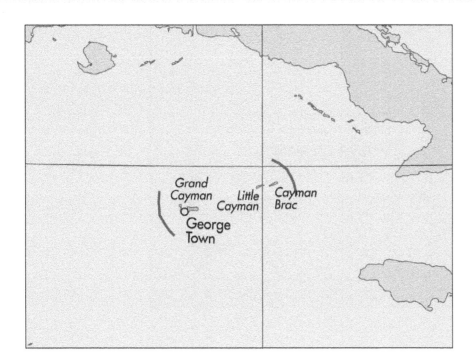

f _____

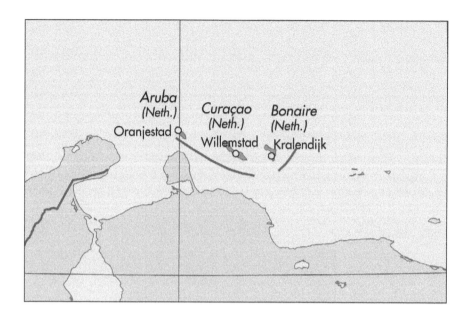

g _____

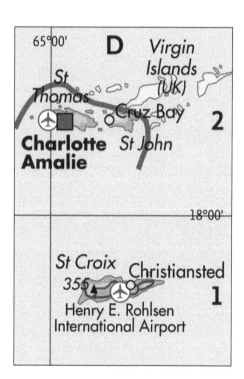

h _____

2 Label the map of the world with the following.

a The names of the seven continents

b The names of the following bodies of water

- Pacific Ocean
- Atlantic Ocean
- Gulf of Mexico
- Indian Ocean
- Southern Ocean
- Arctic Ocean
- Caribbean Sea

c Draw in and label the main lines of latitude and longitude:

- Equator
- Tropic of Cancer
- Tropic of Capricorn

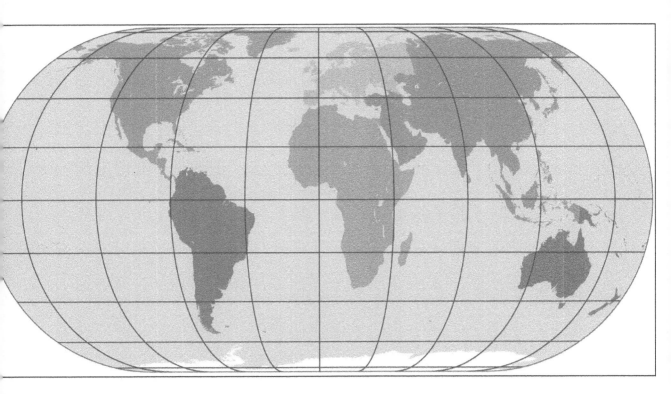

3 Now look at the map you have labelled and answer the questions.

   a Which continent is the largest?

   _____

   b Which continent is the smallest?

   _____

   c Which continent is known as the island continent?

   _____

   d Which ocean is the largest?

   _____

   e Which body of water is enclosed by the Caribbean islands?

   _____

4 Look at the map below. Use coordinates to give the location of the following places.

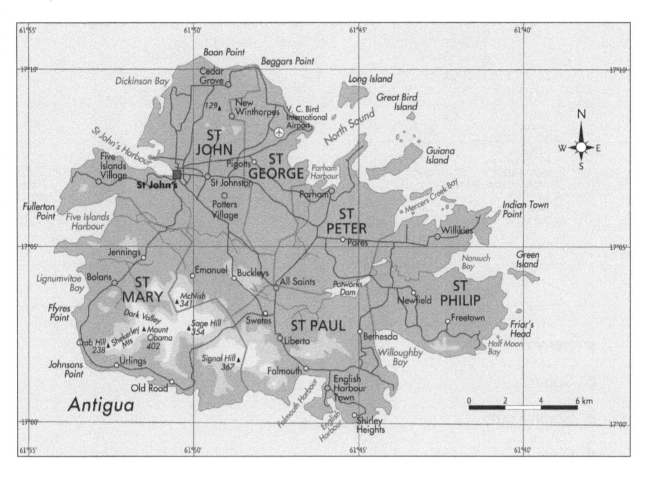

a All Saints _____

b Jennings _____

c Indian Town Point _____

d Freetown _____

e St. John's _____

f Long Island _____

g Crab Hill _____

h Liberta _____

i Half Moon Bay _____

5 Use coordinates to write the location of the countries below the map.

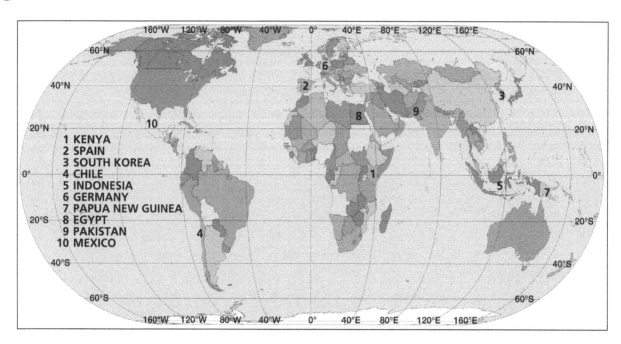

a Kenya _____

b Spain _____

c South Korea _____

d Chile _____

e Indonesia _____

f Germany _____

g Papua New Guinea _____

h Egypt _____

i Pakistan _____

j Mexico _____

6 Using the map below, give the direction to the following places in Antigua.

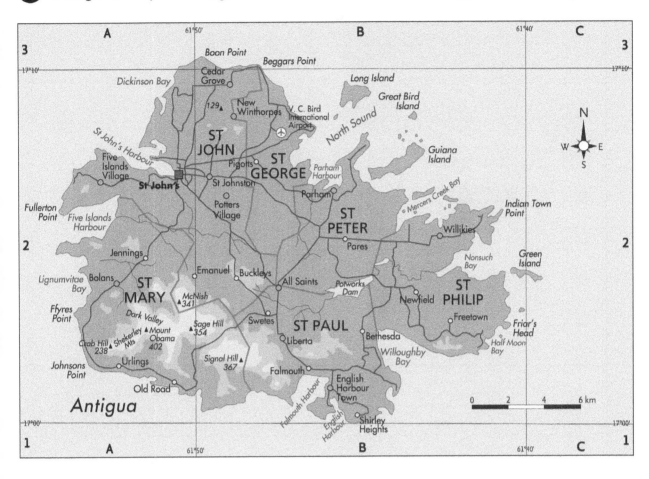

a From All Saints to Potters Village   _____

b From Cedar Grove to Parham   _____

c From Jennings to All Saints   _____

d From Potters Village to St John's   _____

e From Parham to Potworks Dam   _____

f From Shirley Heights to Old Road   _____

g From St. Johns to Falmouth   _____

h From All Saints to Old Road   _____

7 Use the map to answer the following questions about directions.

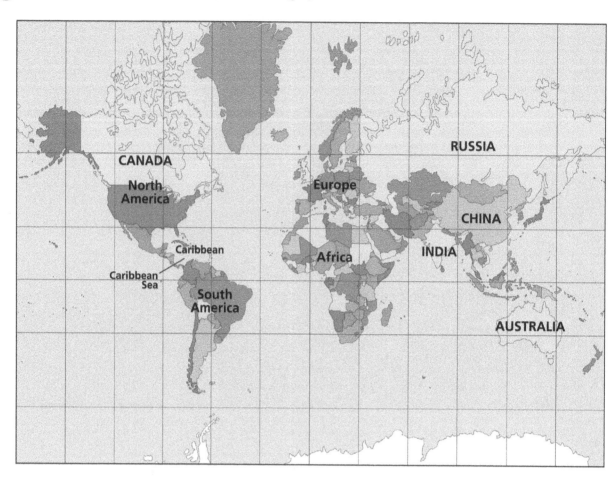

a What direction is North America from South America? _____

b What direction would you travel to get to Australia if
you are currently in China? _____

c What direction is India from South America? _____

d What direction would you have to travel if you are
heading to North America from Africa? _____

e What direction is North America from the
Caribbean Sea? _____

f What direction is Russia from Canada? _____

g What direction is Europe from the Caribbean? _____

8 Use the scale on the map to measure the distances shown.

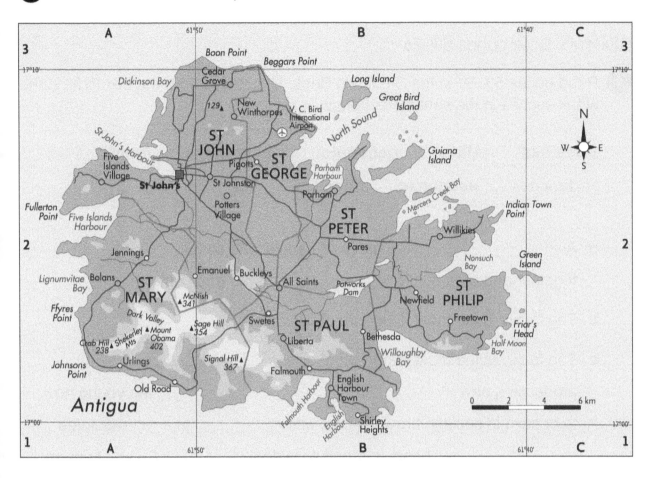

a The distance between Swetes and All Saints   _____

b The distance between Bolans and Potters Village   _____

c The distance between Bethesda and Parham   _____

d The distance between Jennings and Bolans   _____

e The distance between All Saints and Liberta   _____

f The distance between Willikies and Pares   _____

g The distance between Falmouth and Old Road   _____

h The distance between Urlings and Falmouth   _____

i The distance between Cedar Grove and
New Winthorpes   _____

j The distance between Parham and Pares   _____

5 Family

Student's Book pages 53–76

1 Read pages 53–54 in the Student's Book. Use words from the box to fill in the blank spaces in the sentences below.

> sexual   related   generation   institutions   family
>
> teaches   economic   affection   live

a A _____ is a group of people who usually _____ together and are usually _____ to each other.

b The family is the most important of all social _____.

c The family is the most important of all social institutions because it produces a new _____, _____ the young how to behave in society, provides care and _____, regulates _____ behaviour and provides _____ support.

2 Write the name of the type of family shown in each picture.

a

_____

b

c

d

e

3 Complete the crossword. All the words relate to Unit 5 in the Student's Book.

Across

3. Man and woman living together without getting married (6-3)

5. In family terms, this is usually 30 years (10)

7. A group of people who may live together and are related by blood, marriage or another union (6)

8. Family with mother, father and child/children (7)

9. The process where rules, roles and regulations are taught to children (13)

10. Family with more than one generation living under the same roof (8)

Down

1. Family where older brothers and sisters take care of the younger ones (7)
2. The legal union between a man and a woman (8)
4. Gives children their status in society (11)
6. Mother and children and father and children come together to create a family (7)

4 Write a definition for each of the terms below.

a foster family

_____

_____

b adoptive family

_____

_____

c single-parent family

_____

_____

d nuclear family

_____

_____

e blended family

_____

_____

f sibling family

_____

_____

g extended family

_____

_____

h common-law

_____

_____

i marriage

_____

_____

5 In the box are some of the advantages and disadvantages of different types of family. Write each one in the column in the table you think it fits into best.

> The parents are independent.
>
> The house may be overcrowded.
>
> They may live far away from other relatives who could help at times.
>
> Children learn to work together to help each other.
>
> Relationships can be difficult between children, with some resentment.
>
> There are extra adults to help the household run smoothly.
>
> There is usually a close relationship between parent and child.

Single-parent	Nuclear	Blended	Extended	Sibling

6 Read each scenario and then answer the questions that follow.

> **A**
>
> Nuclear family
>
> Since he was in school, Shawn has always wanted to be independent as an adult. He therefore worked hard on his studies. When he left school, he got a job and, by saving carefully, he bought a piece of land on which he built a small house. When he got married, instead of living at his parents' home, he and his wife went to live in his newly-built home. Today, he and his wife and two children live comfortably in their own home.

i   Who are the members of Shawn's family?

_____

ii   What is a nuclear family?

_____

iii What are the possible advantages of living in a nuclear family?

_____

iv What are the possible disadvantages of living in a nuclear family?

_____

_____

B

Extended family

Kemoy was the only son of his family. Ever since he was small he had always believed that his role as the only son would be to look after his parents when they became old and disabled. When Kemoy got married, his wife came to live at his parents' home. Today, his wife and children don't even mention any of the disadvantages of all living in the same house. They are happy in the knowledge that the grandparents willingly provide love and security for all of them. Kemoy and his family know that when the time comes they, too, will care and protect the grandparents, not out of duty, but out of love.

---

i Who are the members of Kemoy's family?

_____

ii What is an extended family?

_____

iii What are some of the situations that may lead to the formation of an extended family?

_____

_____

_____

_____

iv What are the possible advantages of having an extended family?

_____

_____

v What are the possible disadvantages of having an extended family?

_____

_____

C

Single-parent family

Keyshawna was deep in thought. Being a career woman, independent and financially stable, she was thinking of some of the joys she could bring to a child. However, Keyshawna was not interested in getting married. In the end, she decided that she could form a single-parent family by adopting a child. Keyshawna eventually adopted two children and vowed to bring them up as her own.

i What is a single-parent family?

_____

ii Explain some other ways by which a single-parent family may be formed.

_____

_____

iii Give one reason from the passage why Keyshawna did not want to get married.

_____

iv Imagine you are one of Keyshawna's children. Explain what makes you happy in your family and what sometimes makes you unhappy.

_____

_____

_____

v What are some of the difficulties you think Keyshawna might face as a single parent?

_____

_____

_____

D

Sibling family

Jack and Jane were about to celebrate their 35th wedding anniversary. Their four children, ranging from ages 8 to 23 years, were looking forward to it. Then tragedy struck the family, as Jack and Jane were both killed in a car accident. The older children now perform all the functions of their late parents for their younger brothers and sisters in a sibling family.

i What is a sibling family?

_____

ii How are sibling families usually formed?

_____

iii Imagine you are an 11-year-old member of this family. What duties do you think you might be responsible for, to help with the smooth running of the home?

_____

_____

_____

iv What are some of the possible advantages of living in a sibling family?

_____

_____

v What are some possible disadvantages of living in a sibling family?

_____

_____

7 The words in the box are all different functions of the family. Match each one to the correct description.

status   economic   reproduction   love and security
socialisation   protection

a Society depends on the family to create the next generation.

_____

b The members all work together as a team and jointly share their income.

_____

c The family offers physical, economic and psychological support to its members. _____

d Parents pass on their own social identity in terms of race, ethnicity, religion and social class to their children at their birth. _____

e The family provides love and a feeling of safety. _____

f The family teaches the child what the norms are and helps the child to develop their personality before they reach any other group.

_____

8 Read page 65 in the Student's Book. Fill in the table with the roles of the grandparents, parents and children in the family.

Family members	Roles
Parents	
Children	
Grandparents	

9 What are some of the things you do to help your family at home?

_____

_____

_____

_____

_____

_____

_____

_____

10 In the box, draw your family tree showing as many generations as you can. If you need more space, use a separate sheet of paper or a poster board.

11 In your own words, explain each of these social issues that may be faced by a family.

a Domestic abuse

_____

_____

_____

b Child abuse

_____

_____

_____

c Substance abuse

_____

_____

_____

d Divorce

_____

_____

_____

e Teenage pregnancy

_____

_____

_____

12 Read the text in the box then answer the questions below.

> Mrs Thomas, my teacher, said to the class that the family plays an important role in society. She said that each one of us is a member of a family. However, Nichelle complained to the teacher that her family does not spend as much time with each other as they used to.

a Define the term 'family'.

_____

b Give **two** functions of the family.

_____

_____

c Give **one** reason why you think that Nichelle's family may not spend much time with each other.

_____

_____

d Suggest **one** way in which you think Nichelle could try to change the situation.

_____

_____

13 In your own words, explain the United Nations Convention on the Rights of the Child. Use the internet to research five rights of the child that are not in the Student's Book.

_____

_____

_____

_____

_____

_____

_____

_____

_____

_____

_____

_____

_____

14 In your own words, explain some of the things that each of the following institutions can do to help develop strong families.

a School

_____

_____

_____

b Church

_____

_____

_____

c Government

_____

_____

_____

15 Find the words related to Unit 4 below in the wordsearch.

H	B	H	R	H	G	O	U	O	X	H	S	O	Y	S
S	T	R	U	C	T	U	R	E	L	I	G	I	O	N
P	V	E	L	Q	P	E	R	U	T	L	U	C	K	T
V	M	P	F	S	R	R	D	E	O	L	I	G	P	B
J	N	R	Z	K	O	E	O	P	Y	A	E	A	X	C
I	O	O	A	V	C	G	E	T	L	N	F	V	C	I
C	Y	D	I	C	R	U	B	I	E	F	C	H	I	Q
W	Z	U	U	T	E	L	S	R	E	C	I	J	M	P
F	K	C	W	K	A	A	A	C	O	L	T	Z	O	Z
A	S	T	C	Y	T	T	T	D	L	Q	I	N	Q
M	U	I	F	I	I	I	N	R	U	L	E	S	O	R
I	T	O	O	O	O	O	E	E	A	F	N	S	C	N
L	A	N	N	N	N	N	Z	M	I	R	W	C	E	B
Y	T	E	I	C	O	S	T	N	E	R	A	P	T	P
G	S	T	C	H	A	H	P	B	H	S	O	R	A	H

affection   children   culture   economic   family

generation   orientation   parent   procreation

protection   regulations   religion   reproduction

roles   rules   socialisation   society   status

structure